Nervy and frank, hilarious and heart breaking, Sarah Freligh's *Sad Math* vividly captures the worldly naïveté of a girl growing up rebellious in 1950s and 1960s middle America. It is a world of "spit and pearl," where sex mis-education in the classroom, "the clatter / of film unspooling from loop / to loop," the gym teacher who makes it sound "like your tunnel down there is studded with gems so precious you need an armored car in order to make your way safely through the world," is trumped by a cornfield where "[w]e stared at the moon, believing we could see / Neil Armstrong bouncing around from crater / to crater," where they "did it there in the dirt / while everyone and the astronauts watched." "We lit / cigarettes and drove reckless // without seatbelts. We screwed / without condoms, didn't / think twice about the mole / growing on our knee, the arteries / to our hearts silting up with grease," Freligh observes of that era. Evoking an age both oblivious to consequence and intent on meting it out, in *Sad Math* Freligh traces her speaker's coming of age, from an eighth- grade pregnancy and banishment to the Mercy Home for Unwed Mothers, to her new self-described identity as birth mother of a daughter she would not know, ultimately becoming the aging daughter of a mother lost as well, first to mental illness, then to death. "The skeletons will barge out of closets / and riffle through refrigerators for / the tongues they left behind. / Let them speak," Freligh writes, and let them speak she does, in a voice that's vibrant and audacious. Attuned at once to "the Gone [that] will haunt us" and to the power of living fully in the risk of now, Freligh writes for those of us who would "ignore / the lifeguard's warning // […], who run, don't walk," offering in these poems "a song for you / to hum against // the undertow."

—SANDRA MEEK, AUTHOR OF
Road Scatter: Poems

In poems that leap between her mother's dying and her coming of age, of sexuality and psalm, Sarah Freligh navigates her way through the quadratic equation of loss, the algebra of grieving and the calculus of going forward. In this twenty-first century American literary scene of too-often overwritten "projects" or poems with in-house winks and nods to the Academy, this is the kind of streetwise, colloquial, and unapologetically narrative and sometimes ekphrasis poetics I often search for and rarely find. Like her fellow native Detroiter Philip Levine, Freligh makes poems that add guts to heart, subtracts pretense, and divide by the timeless themes of grief and survival. Or as Freligh writes, "I was sixteen and didn't understand / yet how life can kill you a little / at a time. Still, I kissed him back." Against the "hugless, useless / hands dangling from our dumb arms," these are poems that kiss back against the darkness, fiercely.

—SEAN THOMAS DOUGHERTY, AUTHOR OF *All You Ask for Is Longing: New and Selected Poems*

What a fun ride! Working like a Kodacolor flip book, *Sad Math* takes us through growing up in the fifties and sixties, through an unwed teenage pregnancy—with an aftermath of postcards, letters, and lullabies to the daughter given up for adoption—and finally through aging and death. Sarah Freligh's poems are moving, funny, clear, understated, surprising, and superbly detailed. *Sad Math* adds up to a humdinger of a second book.

—RICHARD NEWMAN, AUTHOR OF *All the Wasted Beauty of the World* AND EDITOR OF *River Styx*

Sarah Freligh's *Sad Math* draws you into its black and white, working-class landscape of cigarettes, Kmart parking lots, motels and bars like a slow blues. It's a world that's hollow at its center, an emptied womb, a world emptier still "because we know our babies are not ours at all," because "the Gone will haunt us," because "of loss and its sad math…" One feels taken to a contemporary version of Fitzgerald's valley of ashes, to a place where our Godforsaken can take solace only in the realization that "You are not dead. You are not there yet." Freligh's arresting poems grapple with the math, show the work, and attempt to substantiate a blue-collar past in a way that makes better sense than did the experience of living it.

—JOHN HOPPENTHALER,
AUTHOR OF *Domestic Garden*

Sarah Freligh's *Sad Math* catalogs loss: lost jobs and homes and habits, lost loves and lives and selves. There are not enough poems that do what these poems do, confronting ugly truths with humor and heart. You can't help but root for their speakers, among them a country club waitress, a mall photographer, an unwed mother, and a grieving daughter. Freligh knows too well the many ways "the Gone will haunt us," but she finds the music in memory, with all its subtractions and divisions.

—CAKI WILKINSON,
AUTHOR OF *The Wynona Stone Poems*

Sad Math

Sarah Freligh

MOON CITY PRESS
Department of English
Missouri State University
901 South National Avenue
Springfield, Missouri 65897

The story contained herein is a work of fiction. All incidents, situations, institutions, governments, and people are fictional, and any similarity to characters or persons living or dead is strictly coincidental.

First Edition
Copyright © 2015 by Sarah Freligh
All rights reserved.
Published by Moon City Press, Springfield, Missouri, USA, in 2015.

Library of Congress Cataloging-in-Publication Data

Freligh, Sarah.
Sad math: poems / Sarah Freligh.
Further Library of Congress information is available upon request.

ISBN-10: 0-913785-64-4
ISBN-13: 978-0-913785-64-5

Cover art: *Marceline Ticket Booth* by Sarah Williams, oil on board, 30 by 30 inches, 2014

Text edited by Sara Burge and copyedited by Karen Craigo.
Cover and interior designed by Charli Barnes.

Author photo by Walter Colley Images.

Manufactured in the United States of America.

www.mooncitypress.com

For Bruce L. Ruesink
and Veronica Kornberg:
ideal readers

ACKNOWLEDGMENTS

Thanks to my family and my friends, especially Darby Knox, Jennifer Litt, Charlie Cote, Joan Pedzich, Anne Panning, and the Gang at Ashland for the wine and for your insightful comments on the work.

Thanks to mentors and teachers: Kim Addonizio, David Mason, Pete Fairchild, Stephen Haven, Ruth L. Schwartz, Kathryn Winograd, Mark Irwin, and Angie Estes.

Thanks to Sara Burge and Mike Czyzniejewski at Moon City Press for all you do.

Thanks finally to the National Endowment for the Arts, whose generous grant helped me begin these poems.

Grateful acknowledgment is made to the editors of the following journals in which these poems, or earlier versions of them, first appeared:

Barn Owl Review: "Blissfield, Michigan" (as "Blissfield, Michigan: July 1969") and "In the Bones"

Brevity: "A Brief Natural History of an Eighth Grade Girl"

burntdistrict: "Lullaby for the Daughter I Gave Away"

Connotation Press: An Online Artifact: "A Letter to You About Myself," "Pilgrims," and "Starting With an Old Photo of My Mother and Ending on a Hill"

Ducts: "And Then I Blew It," "Him to Her: 1969," "In the Psych Ward, My Mother Thinks," and "What I've Lost"

Louisville Review: "My Friend" and "The Beginning of Something Is Always the End of Another"

Naugatuck River Review: "In Which I Imagine a Stray Cat as Ulysses"

The Prose-Poem Project: "Postcard from the Lower Peninsula, Circa 1958"

Phat'itude: "Class of '69: Page from a Yearbook" as "Class of '69"

Provincetown Arts: "The Birth Mother to Her Daughter on Her First Birthday"

Rattle: "Sex Education"

The Sun Magazine: "Donut Delite: 1969," "Safe," and "Wondrous"

Verse Daily: "Lullaby for the Daughter I Gave Away"

Some of the poems appeared as a chapbook, *A Brief Natural History of an American Girl,* published by Accents Publishing in 2012.

"We Smoke" was the winner of *Sycamore Review*'s 2015 Flashcard Contest.

The following poems have appeared in these anthologies:

- "Waitress," in *Raising Lilly Ledbetter: Women Poets Occupy the Workspace*, ed. Caroyne Wright (Lost Horse Books, 2015)

- "The Class of '69" in *Death Poems*, ed. Russ Kick (Disinformation Books: Red Wheel/Weiser Press, 2013)

- "Old Flame," *1 x 8 x 16: Sixteen Poets Respond to Brittany Ryan*, ed. Steven Huff (Big Pencil Press, 2012)

- "December" as "The Tenth of December," *Bigger Than What They Seem: An Anthology of Short Poems*, ed. Katerina Stoykova Klemer (Accents Publishing, 2011)

TABLE OF CONTENTS

One

STARTING WITH AN
OLD PHOTO OF MY MOTHER
AND ENDING ON A HILL

She is red-lipped and slender in a shirt-
waist dress, bun of hair hidden
under a white hat. She lives
on ice chips and cigarettes.
Chopin is in the fingers
that twine through mine, a warning
and an endearment. My brother's
a shifting load on her hip. I will grow up
and smoke cigarettes the way she did, in lieu
of food, hungrily tap my ashes into
a ceramic whale, belly hollowed out
where its womb would have been.

I will never wear her clothes.

Sometimes I drive south on two-lane highways
through one-light towns until I'm cradled
in hills. In August, the maple trees are dying
inside. The chlorophyll's stopped rising and soon
enough the leaves will yellow. I think of her
body as one of those small towns where the lone
factory's down to a single shift, a building where birds
fly in and out of deciduous windows and high school
boys break and enter nightly to light fires and talk
big. Listen to them and you can almost believe
their hearts will never turn bitter and quit.

I'd write a love poem to those boys, but I wouldn't
know where to send it so I'm saying this to you,
Mom, shouting from a hilltop at a couple
of cows who look up at me and go on chewing.
They're as blank as grief can be, the emptiness
of a parking lot ten minutes after the shift's
let out, a dandelion in the cracked
asphalt waving at the trail of exhaust
from the last car to leave.

POSTCARD FROM THE LOWER PENINSULA, CIRCA 1958

Your father drives silent and one-handed, crooked left
elbow riding on the window's rim. Your mother picks
skin from her cuticles. You and your sister sprawl in back
like badly packed luggage, make faces at the skein of cars
unraveling behind you. In Michigan, roads lead only to
other roads: same dotted white line, eternal border of corn
and cows. You drive and drive and are never there.

You eat lunch at a rickety picnic table near a hill in the
road where trucks grind by, farting exhaust. Your tuna
sandwich tastes gassy; your Dixie cup of lemonade is hot
as pee. Flies helicopter over a steaming pile of poop your
parents pretend not to see. Your sister whispers you'll
likely die from bad mayonnaise in an hour or so.

Hours later, your father drives silent and two-handed.
Your mother picks her lip. Your sister is asleep. You are
not dead. You are not there yet.

THEIRSTORY [Notes on a Script]

At twenty she stands arm in arm with two other girls

on a dock over a long-forgotten lake

wearing a pinch-waist bathing suit that

[*I bet is red because she looked so good in red*]

is gray in the black-and-white photo the way

history is always black and white and filled

with rows of women—gray-faced, no-name

women—bent over sewing machines or sitting

elbow to elbow with my mother at the telephone

company fast hands connecting callers

[*soprano chorus of* Number please *revved up and frantic at 78 rpm*]

even as a knife of static stabs the news from London,

the war the men have all marched off to and when

the fighting ends in a white-out of confetti and a mile-long

conga line my father will wrap his nightmares

[*of burned bodies, the shrieks of the almost dead*]

in plastic, hang them behind his Navy blues in the back

of the closet, kiss my mother good-bye before he whistles

out each morning in a gray flannel suit

[*so very Cary Grant*]

into a Technicolor world where the sky is

[*turquoise*]

the limit for a smart guy like him, his oyster

with its promise of spit and pearl, a world

she almost starred in way back when.

THOSE DAYS

I imagine a crowd gathered
in front of Gray's Floor Covering
to watch the ambulance pull away

—red light still, siren quiet—
and figured there was nothing
anyone could do for Waylon Gray.

The news caught fire
at that afternoon's
choir practice, jumped

from row to row,
soprano to alto:
Patty's dad is dead

the only way a father left us
in those days, a sheet
on a stretcher, feet

first, exiting a showroom
where only seconds ago
he was slicing tile

or figuring the price
on a square footage
of purple shag, no

warning before his heart leapt
like a fish and tangled
in the rotted net of his chest.

DONUT DELITE

All summer I tossed wheels of dough
into a sea of grease where they browned
and crisped while I smoked half
a cigarette. By the time the owner
stopped by, the air was humid with sugar,
the bakery cases filled with rows
of doughnuts I'd frosted and sprinkled.
He'd pull a buck from his wallet to pay
for his cruller, his cup of coffee, show me
the photo of his son squinting into the light,
smiling like a man who didn't know
he would die at Khe Sanh.

On my last day the boss pressed
a wad of bills into my hand and kissed me
good-bye. When he slipped
his tongue into my mouth,
I could feel the old dog
of his heart rear up and tug
at its leash. His breath tasted
like ashes. He was my father's friend.
I was sixteen and didn't understand
yet how life can kill you a little
at a time. Still, I kissed him back.

SEX EDUCATION

How is it I recall so exactly the clatter
of film unspooling from loop
to loop, the musk of perfume radiating

from my wrists and throat, the warm gush
of Juicy Fruit, the rasp of stockings
as we crossed and uncrossed our legs. The heat

in that room, a flock of girls cooped up
away from the roosters, the almost-men
of our fantasies who we dreamed

would stand beneath our windows
one day and crow for us as Romeo
had for Juliet. How we laughed

when an army of sperm ejected
from a cannon into a body
of water where they swam or died,

cartoon smiles disappearing in tiny peeps
as one by one they drowned, leaving
one last lonely sperm to swim up

the long isthmus where the river
opened to an ocean, and I still recall
how the orchestra soared as he swam

and swam toward the round ship
of the egg, and how we stood
and cheered when he docked, exhausted

and triumphant, this tiny survivor,
this sturdy sperm we would spend
the next ten years trying to kill off,

and because of the stupid movie I felt
like a murderer each time I imagined him battering
frantic and headlong against the barrier

I'd erected down there, shouting
Defense de la defense! as he died in spasms
of agony and once—because I was drunk

and didn't give a damn, because I wanted
only to sink into the soft chance of carelessness—
I let the whole bunch of them skinny-dip

without a death sentence of chemicals
awaiting them at the end of their swim
and because I'd forgotten what

my teacher told us that day
after the film ended and the lights came up:
Remember, girls, it takes just one.

What chance did I have? They
were as fit as Olympians, as cunning
as spies. They came in formation,

in armies, entire Caesar's legions, coming
and coming and coming   always
so many of them and one of me.

AND THEN I BLEW IT

What did I know about sex? Nothing
but what I'd learned in eighth-grade
health class: the proper names
for private parts I located
and labeled on a cartoon girl:
her uterus a lima bean, ovaries a pair
of acorns pinioned in the twin trunks
of her fallopian tubes. I aced every quiz
that year but knew nothing
of the body, its boggy smells and odd
topographies, though I pretended to,
like a tourist who'd experienced Paris
through a car window. What did I know
about *blow job*? I understood it literally
as an occupation. My first night at work
I surveyed all of his avenues and alleys, mapped
every crack and bump. I kissed him
pink, held on a high whole note, long
enough to set every dog in town to howling.

SHUT UP, PLEASE,
I'M SPEAKING

of love. You remember. We made it
once in a crummy motel near Binghamton

while snow fell, four inches in an hour.
The curtains gapped, admitting a slice

of light that cut your back in half while
all night clouds shaped like potatoes

floated across the TV screen. Afterward
you untangled the sheet from our feet,

rolled wordless into sleep leaving me
to stare at your back, smooth as the motel

soap fresh from the wrapper. Like love
was before I said it out loud and someone

in the next room fisted the wall, shouted
at me to please shut the fuck up.

A BRIEF NATURAL HISTORY
OF AN EIGHTH-GRADE GIRL

*The males [of many animal species] … continue to
vie for the prize of siring offspring via the one-celled
messengers of themselves they leave as a consequence of
mating: their sperm.* [1]

Fuck is everywhere, scrawled in black felt pen on the stall
walls of the third floor girls' room or chalked across the
red brick near the bus line where the greaser boys mob like
crows. You walk past them daily, a fifty-yard trudge from car
to entrance, and the entire time, you feel their eyes radaring
through your wool kilt down to where your white Lollipop
panties hide your treasure chest. At least that's how your
gym teacher makes it sound, like your tunnel down there is
studded with gems so precious you need an armored car in
order to make your way safely through the world. Like you
should die rather than hand over the key.

*… among insects and spiders, at least, … females control
much of what happens in reproduction.* [2]

In the locker room after swim class, you huddle up with a
dozen other girls underneath the hair dryer—a rusted udder
whose nipples blow tornadoes of hot air at your scalp—and
howl the lyrics to "Louie Louie" into the bristles of your

---

[1]Marlene Zuk, "Sperm and Eggs on Six Legs,"
Natural History 119, no. 6 (June 2011): 23–35

[2]Ibid.

hairbrush. You try not to look shocked when the girl next to you brags about almost-but-not-quite getting finger-fucked by a tenth-grader in his father's garage, or when she sweeps her hair up to show you two faded blue stains where he sucked her neck.

> *… female black field crickets in Australia let*
> *spermatophores remain attached longer for more*
> *attractive males (those singing energetic songs) than for*
> *relatively wimpy males.*[3]

At night you manufacture movies in your head starring you and whatever face you paste onto a shifting cast of fantasy men—the cute lead singer for Herman's Hermits, usually, or any one of the Dave Clark Five. Or the skinny ninth-grader whose AV duties endow him with a spoonful of cool evident in the ease with which he threads filmstrip into projector. In your own movie, he threads your treasure chest with gold and asks you to do it, only you don't know enough about it to even imagine it, and so you fall asleep.

> *… females of most species mate with more than one male,*
> *often in rapid succession …*[4]

Practice makes perfect and over the years you will practice a lot. You will do it in motel rooms and basement apartments and once on the eighteenth green of a golf course on Christmas Eve. You will do it with men you call friends, with men you see once and never again, and men who are not nice. You will do it so often that you will barely recall the time before you understood what it entailed, only that it loomed in

---

[3] Ibid.

[4] Ibid.

the distance like a city at night and how you counted down
the miles until you arrived.

> *Leigh W. Simmons, a biologist at the University of*
> *Western Australia, in Perth, claims that you don't*
> *understand life unless you have studied dung flies ...[5]*

---

[5]Ibid.

BLISSFIELD, MICHIGAN

We stared at the moon, believing we could see
Neil Armstrong bouncing around from crater
to crater, even Sue who'd called it all a crazy

hoax, a stunt taking place on the Hollywood
sound stage where they used to shoot *The Mickey
Mouse Club*. We wandered into a cornfield

and got high again and tried to find the rum
Sam had hidden that afternoon and when we
got tired, we lay on the ground and stared some

more at the sky. Billy ran his hand up my thigh
and I said stop though I felt lit up, all green
as in go, and when I'd run out of nos, I

rolled over and did it there in the dirt
while everyone and the astronauts watched.

HIM TO HER: 1969

Summer before last I parked cars at
the country club—high-class rides with seats
softer than a baby's face, as wide as beds.
Men in white dinner jackets dropped tips
in my palm, told me to watch myself
with their brand new Caddies or else.
My boss called me *kid* if we weren't busy,
Hey, asshat when we were, threw keys
at me. I used to pretend those cars were mine
and the world was my kingdom: the dimes
riding heavy in my pocket, the wives
who smelled of smoke and roses, the chime
of ice against glass, the sprinklers tossing
silvery coins of water to the grateful grass.

SAFE

After we buried my mother,
we drank beer and told stories
in the room where she died.

The hospital bed was gone
and the portable commode
I'd helped her settle on, love

seat tucked flush with the window,
long sofa shoved against the wall
like always, the same sofa where she'd fall

asleep watching baseball while she waited
for me to come home from some high school date.
Once when I wasn't back by midnight,

she threw a raincoat over her flannel pajamas,
drove around until she found me
mussed and unbuttoned behind

the Big Boy sharing a bagged can
of Colt .45 with the second-string
quarterback. All the way

home and for an entire week, I was punished
by silence. The last time I saw her,
I wanted her to speak to me, tell me

she wasn't really asleep, to lock
the front door, turn off the last
light, follow me upstairs

having made the house safe
for the night but she didn't
know who I was.

WOMAN'S WORK

Sylvia: I've read you tidied
your kitchen before you died:

scrubbed the egg crust
from fork tines, sudsed

and rinsed your china teacup,
dried them both by hand.

You knew gas was best: no mess.
My mother never talked

about the time she went
crazy and away for a week.

She knew the courage
of shutting up, a shut

door, exquisite click
of lock. After meals,

she liked to polish
the kitchen counter

until the white Formica gleamed
her face back up at her.

Seeing herself
she rubbed harder.

IN THE PSYCH WARD, MY MOTHER THINKS

a zinc pig is God.
Witness this rosary

of ants, black beads strung
along a linoleum floor.

How a broom splinters,
breaks.

How the chrome bumper gave
her back her face.

How blood smells, a root
cellar in winter.

Two

NOTES ON
"Mother Holding Child,"
KODACOLOR PRINT, CIRCA 1952

[1]The mother is holding the child on the left side of her body, a position consistent with works by Giotto and Fra Angelico, Italian artists of the fourteenth and fifteenth centuries, both of whom painted the Christ Child on the left side of the Virgin Mary. Salk (1960, 1961, 1962, 1973) argues that by holding the infant on the left side, the mother places the infant in proximity to the beat of her heart, thereby calming the child and reassuring the mother. Indeed, the child in this photograph seems tranquil to the point of sleepiness.

[2]The mother is dressed in a style of clothing consistent with the period, a classic shirtwaist dress informed by Dior's "New Look" of the late 1940s and early 1950s. Note the hyperfeminine silhouette, how the skirt's deep pleating creates the illusion of full hips and a pinched-in waist (although it's likely the mother is wearing a girdle or long-line bra to achieve the look and will not breathe deeply until sleep where she will dream of apples).

[3]The mother is smiling down at the child, a pose evocative of paintings where Mary gazes at the Christ Child.

[4]The fading is typical of Kodacolor prints of this era, caused by unstable magenta dye-forming color couplers that remained in the prints after processing. Wilhelm (1993) refers to this period as "The Totally Lost Kodacolor Era of 1942-1953" and estimates that hundreds of millions, perhaps billions, of Kodacolor prints and negatives have not survived.

[5]The mother's hair is pulled back into a ponytail, a style favored by busy young mothers during this period for its ease as well as its evocation of youth.

[6]The mother and child stand alone in a large vacant lot, a composition that both suggests and underscores the isolation common among mid-twentieth century women confined to their homes by young children. It was during this period that the previously agrarian landscape was largely bulldozed to make way for massive postwar suburban development. City records show the lot in question had been an apple orchard.

[7]A newspaper obituary (*Daily Telegram*, April 27) lists the cause of death for the mother as cancer, one of 549,838 deaths by cancer in 1999 (American Cancer Society).

[8]A shadow in the photo's lower-right corner appears to be the toe of a man's dress shoe. Microscopic inspection reveals a charred stump.

[9]One sixty-fourth of a second. Yellow. Yellowing.

[10]The child holds the mother in her heart.

THE BIRTH
MOTHER ON THE
DAY AFTER

My stitches pinched. The pad
bunched between my legs,
leaked blood all over
my underpants.
My jeans wouldn't zip.
All I could take away
from that place fit
into a paper bag.

In the car, my mother lit
a cigarette and said
she thought it best
if we put this mess
behind us. I said
OK. My stitches
itched. The stoplight
stuck on red.

WE SMOKE

We smoke because the nuns say we shouldn't—he-man Marlboros or Salems, slender and meadow fresh, over cups of thin coffee at the Bridge Diner. We fill an ashtray in an hour easy while Ruby the waitress marries ketchups and tells us horror stories about how her first labor went on for fifty-two hours until her boy was yanked out of her butt first and now she has this theory that kids who come out like that got their brains in their asses from Day One. She says we're smart to give our babies away to some Barbie-and-Ken couple with a house and a yard with real grass and a swing set, and we nod like we agree with her and smoke some more.

Nights we huddle up under the bathroom window in the Mercy Home for Unwed Mothers and blow smoke at the stained sky while we swap stories about our babies doing handstands on our bladders, playing volleyball with our hearts, how our sons will be presidents or astronauts, and our daughters will be beautiful and chaste, and because we know our babies are not ours at all, we talk about everything and nothing while we watch a moth bang up against the light and smoke some more.

EASY

And when a cop caught me naked
from the waist up the night
I parked with a boy behind

a construction site, high beams
of my bare breasts white
as the bra wadded up

on the console, the dress
I sewed that afternoon
tossed over the front seat

now, zipper's whisk the sound
my scissors had made on first
cut, crisp and final, I gave him

a fake name, *Renee*, because
it sounded appropriately
slutty, a girl who'd carry

rubbers in her purse, cover up
her discomfort by laughing
at the cop who flicked

his flashlight off out of some
sense of decorum or maybe
because he had a daughter

the same age as me, would want
a fellow cop to be easy
on her. Hope is a dress

I assembled from three yards
of cotton, fashioned a self
to step into, and here I was

already without it.

MORNING PRAYER
IN THE MERCY
HOME FOR UNWED
MOTHERS

Sister Bernadette shouts
from the pulpit about chastity

and the healing power
of repentance, how our bodies

should be vessels for the Lord
instead of receptacles for

young men with lust in their loins.
Forgive me, Father, but piety

makes me tired. Yesterday
I yawned my way

through the Lord's Prayer
and got caught: Fifteen demerits

and extra KP for me, potatoes
probably because I hate them so.

I bow my head and dream
of the moment I'll unfasten

my bra and sink like a stone
into bed, the second I'll cup

the swell of my stomach, ripe
as paradise, and try to say

my name the way he did
right after he called out

to God and claimed
that territory for himself.

THE BIRTH MOTHER
ON HER DAUGHTER'S
FIRST BIRTHDAY

It's late and the woman one cell over
is finally quiet. Awake, she's a cocked
fist, fights sleep when it threatens
to take her down for the night,
struggling and punching the thin
sheets to keep what she imagines
is hers. The guard says it's snowing
—*a real sonofabitch to drive in*—
a foot already and more to fall.
On our first date, your father
drove to the Kmart parking lot
and made figure eights in the new
snow. I sat in the passenger's seat
and said *Go faster* because I liked
how his biceps looked
under his flannel shirt
when he yanked that steering wheel
and made that car obey him.

I should tell you
everyone's innocent
in here. Guilt is a nametag we wear
for therapy sessions, tear up
and discard on the way out.
We sit in a circle and drink
bitter coffee, tell stories
that scald the tongue.
The day you were born you felt
like a bowl of hot pasta the doctor
spilled on my stomach. The nurse said
Your baby is beautiful but she was wrong.
You looked like Eisenhower,
and you were never mine,
just something I might
have borrowed for a while.

A LETTER TO YOU ABOUT MYSELF

I still do bad things. Sometimes I bite my fingernails, not down
to the quick, but only to even out the rough spots. Last week my
thumb snagged a new pair of tights. All day the run laddered up
my thigh, displaying beige leg flesh in each little window. I'm always
in a hurry, an hour ahead of the here and now, a refugee from my own
life. I hope I didn't give that to you. My teeth are bad, maybe yours
are, too? My dentist says I'll be lucky to keep the teeth I have as if he
knows what my future will be: me in a hospital bed cranked up high
enough to see outdoors: the birds fighting for the last bit of seed
in the feeder. The drone of a TV across the hall, a soap opera whose
characters I no longer recognize. The names are the same, the actors
different. Every day is like this. The girl who brings my tray is not
the one from yesterday though she says she is. Her hands are hard
and strong. *Here's your boiled egg, honey*, she says. I don't answer
to that name anymore.

THE BIRTH MOTHER
CELEBRATES
INDEPENDENCE DAY, 1976

My neighbor downstairs sunbathes
in a red bikini on a faded chaise lounge,
the scar on her stomach grinning
up at me from beneath the nose
of her navel. Her baby's three now;
he squeals naked through the sprinkler
while she chain-smokes Salems
and shouts at him to stay away
from the teenagers, their bottle
rockets and cherry bombs. She
works at a bar up the road, serving
shots and beer to truckers who stuff
her tip jar with bills, propose to her
when drunk. The walls are thin. I hear
her hum to herself while she fixes
dinner, sing to her son while she bathes
him, songs in a language only they understand.
Later I'll watch her grill hot dogs
on a hibachi. She'll wait
until dark to light sparklers, show
her boy how to write his name
on the blank check of night sky.

THE BEGINNING OF
SOMETHING IS ALWAYS
THE END OF ANOTHER

Take the day, for instance: How the ruff
of sun's first light shoulders the night

aside and when I butt my morning
cigarette, my absolute last cigarette,

I begin to chew my cuticles and why
my next-door neighbor drops by

daily to cry about her ex who ran off
with some little slut he met in tango class,

and when my twenty-year-old cat
misses the litter box, howls at

headlights that strafe the ceiling,
I know this will end in ashes

at a cemetery where we stood
over my mother's urn, hugless, useless

hands dangling from our dumb arms
while on the hill above us a guy wearing

soiled khakis lounged in a golf cart,
waiting for us to understand this was it,

the end, we needed to leave already
so he could finally begin to dig.

THE BIRTH MOTHER
AT WORK IN J.C. PENNEY'S
PORTRAIT STUDIO

I twist bits of tissue into a frog or fish
make them dance for the toddlers frightened
by the lights, the shrieking babies with
their glistening holes. My boss says no one

calms the children like I do, not even Edie
who likes to brag the first babies she shot
are in high school now, as if daring me
to ask her whether she likes her job or not.

I stay low to the ground, try not to move
too loud or fast, an alien in this paradise
of fake flowers and grape lollipop love

doled out by Mom. Through camera's lens,
I see what might have been: all grabby
hands and sticky lips. Eternity.

LULLABY FOR THE
DAUGHTER I GAVE AWAY

—after Beckian Fritz Goldberg's "Retro Lullaby"

Sometimes I write a letter of resignation to the universe
    and sometimes I forget to stamp the envelope, never
    without an argument. I used to believe

fact and truth were the same thing
    though I learned to lie without smiling
    after I had the waitress dream—ten tables
    of golfers shouting for martinis—

and now all I have is a picture of an old castle.

If I pin the picture above my desk,
    the prince will turn into a handsome frog
    and he will grow a backbone and learn how
    to leap when I call him.

And I'll whisper, *It's OK, you can save me.*
    Be my sex.

I can never remember what to call him.

In fact, my father said I'd end up with a toad, a
    cold-blooded croaker. My mother used to say
    that if they drained the swamp, I'd find
    a date for the prom if I wasn't
    too picky. I moved out soon after.

Tragic, she said, to have a daughter who never writes home.

But now, at last, I've mucked
    through that swamp, arrived spry
    as a froglet at the altar of my desk
    and I forget I'm still wet and cold,
    I can't grasp a pen and if I could

I wouldn't write home. But if I did, I'd say,
    I'm OK, you can forget me. You can be
    my heavy bag.

Someday, I'll be a sore hip,
    invisible. Because the
    ink on the letter is black and forever
    and someone

will read them out loud, the Gone will haunt us

and the skeletons will barge out of closets
    and riffle through refrigerators for
    the tongues they left behind.

Let them speak. You can be my frog, my toad, my letter home.
    My baby. My return address.

LAST LETTER TO YOU
WHEREVER YOU ARE

Night is falling but you are not at home
to hear how loud the sky sounds when
its canopy collapses and rains down
parts of stars, a bruise of moon; how
frightening the light looks spilling
into the room, gallons of moon ruining
the wood floor. The man in my TV
points to a red stain spreading across
a map and tells me it's best to stay
inside but there's a hole in the roof
over what used to be my bed and words
racketing my head. Love, I pray you're safe
inside a hem in the horizon where
night has not fallen so hard as here.

IN THE BONES

1

The phlebotomist ties me off and swabs me, says he
doesn't have to slap me. *You have beautiful veins,* he says.
Look there, how they pop right up for me.

2

Blood: Cells suspended in plasma. Considered a
specialized form of connective tissue, given its origin in
the bones.

3

I sold my blood once: pint for twenty dollars, a single
limp bill. I bought a sweater ribbed at the midriff and
wore it with jeans to a kegger in the basement of a
fraternity house. Sipped beer from a plastic cup and went
home with the second-string quarterback. We shared a
joint. Pink Floyd made me dizzy. I fell asleep and woke
to my sweater folded under my head.

4

He's done this thousands of times, swears he can do it
in his sleep, this in and out, this invasion. He one-hands
Band-Aids, grabs two tubes, a wad of cotton. *Hold it,* he
says, while he busies himself with labels.

5

You will never forget her hand, a dimpled starfish, fingers
a smaller version of yours. Already she was someone else's,
wrapped in a pink blanket for delivery. The name you gave
her was temporary. Did she/does she bite her nails until
they bleed?

6

Blood is thick, iron hard. Think of magnets, the pull of
them. Whoever is infused with my blood will be drawn to
me, a millimeter at a time. You must believe it can happen.

Three

THE CLASS OF '69:
PAGE FROM A YEARBOOK

The dead live on, black-
framed faces airbrushed
of acne, their eulogies
woven from a warp of truth,
the woof of exaggeration. Who

knew the girl that died of leukemia
swung snakes like lariats
and writhed with the fever
of Jesus on Sunday. Or the quiet boy
in the dark tie and starched shirt

whose head was sheared clean
from his neck one night when he drove
drunk under an oncoming semi—
who knew he spent
his last hour throwing ten-dollar bills

at an old stripper named
Miss Cherry Blossom. Who knew
he laughed when she picked
them up in the crack of her ass.
Who knew how bad blood

cells multiply, gang up
on the good ones. Who knew
about Pavlov's dog, the tuning fork
and the promise of food. We lit
cigarettes and drove reckless

without seat belts. We screwed
without condoms, didn't
think twice about the mole
growing on our knee, the arteries
to our hearts silting up with grease.

We bent over a light table
framing photos in small coffins
of black tape to honor
the dead, the legendary dead,
about whom we knew nothing.

MY FRIEND

Your cat's quit eating the food
you left me, even the sliced beef

you said he adored. He sits
by his water bowl and waits

for you, like you're hiding,
sniffs a visitor's pants hem

maybe believing you're residing
in that inch of real estate. Like him,

I sense you everywhere. Yesterday
at the mall I waved at a woman who was you

before the chemo charred
the hair from your head. She laughed

past me. I pretended
interest in a window

full of skinny mannequins sporting
pastel short-shorts. I see you

at twenty-four. I see you
as the woman wearing

purple, bent over a cane, the old
we used to talk about, the foreign

country you'll never visit
with me. I'll send you

a postcard when I get there
wishing you were here.

I think your cat's sitting
shiva, grieving the way

I will when I no longer
see you everywhere.

GEOGRAPHY

On a long-ago Sunday, I spun
the dial on the car radio
to rinse the starch from

the Episcopal hymnal with
a little Motown just as
Jack Ruby pulled a pistol

from his coat. A president
waved from a blue convertible
while I stared at a wall map

of the Soviet Union, a giant cape
draped over the shoulders
of two continents, generations

before it unraveled into a tatter
of countries ending in -stan.
The moment my mother slips soft

from this life, I'm thinking about
dinner and cat litter, not the Great
Lakes and three states that separate

us. Uzbekistan. Baghdad.
Buffalo. Dallas. My atlas
is old, the paper's fading.

IN THE OLYMPICS
OF GRIEF

my mother's death nets
a score no higher than five. Zero

grandkids. Age had silvered
her hair, no style points there

and further deduction for
the liver cancer that blew

her gut up yellow until
it killed her, a blessing

in the eyes of those funeral
folks who shook my hand

and said how lovely
God was to call her home.

Some cancers are just sexier
than others, low-cut

and sequined in a roomful
of black, long-sleeved leotards.

Amos's son died
of a fast-moving melanoma

at eighteen—chemo starved
the meat from his bones, singed

the hair from his head yet
he grew more beautiful.

Judges love the dead who go
so gracefully and young. Ask

Janice whose mother flails on
at a hundred and one, half

blind and meaner than speed.
Her life's an eternal trial,

her death a finish line
everybody's rooting for. She'll

be a zero in the Olympics of grief,
not worth a single trumpet, one

note of an anthem, the energy
you'd expend to raise a flag.

ROUTINE

The hour after my cat died, I swam laps
                because it was Monday and because
I'd read that routine is an antidote

to grief and my routine for nearly nine years
                had been to swim at noon on Monday
and Wednesday, sometimes Sunday,

though I'd felt guilty on the days
                my cat meowed around the house,
a rag of bones, yet somehow

I kept swimming, whispering
                I'm sorry, I'm sorry because under water
the loudest sound is the absence of sound

not of my cat as he sighed into death
                or my mother who died silent the second
my dad turned to talk to the hospice nurse

who dressed my mom in a green sweatsuit
                and sent her off to be cremated, same
as my cat. My mother came back

in a silver urn, my cat in a metal box
                bordered by roses, his name
typed and taped to the bottom.

PILGRIMS

Two men from the halfway house
are hanging out on the corner,
shin deep in ragged snow
tagged by a graffiti of dog pee
and car dirt. Their words turn
to steam but they don't talk
much, don't do much of anything
but stand on the corner in their thin
shoes, hands jammed into jacket
pockets as afternoon trudges on
toward evening, the blue hour
when bars blaze awake in a hum
of neon. Somewhere in the wrecked
cities this pair of pilgrims has left
behind, a communion of drinkers
is gathering on stools, thirsty
for whiskey's swift benediction,
sung back by a silver choir
of bottles, but look
how the tall man bends
his face to the cupped hands
of the short man
offering a match. See him
tip his head back to exhale,
let the dime-sized flakes
bless his face.

IN WHICH
I IMAGINE A STRAY
CAT AS ULYSSES

He appears twice daily, at eight
a.m. and later on in the blue hour

after the horizon has swallowed the sun.
Swaggers up the porch steps and waits

for me to serve him. Grunts approval,
complains when I'm late. He's dust-

whiskered, streaked with grease
from junkyard odysseys. His nose

is scarred, hard souvenir of an epic
battle for a minute's tryst with a thin

calico. Nights he doesn't show, I leave
the light on, sit by the window. Knit.

DECEMBER

On the fire escape, one
stupid petunia still blooms,
purple trumpet blowing
high notes at the sky long
after the rest of the band
has packed up
and gone home.

MY FATHER AT NINETY

is stubborn, hell bent on walking
an hour every day in any weather
so I measure my pace to his
side-to-side lurch. It's Christmas,

thirty-nine degrees and rain
turning to sleet, my socks soggy,
blisters blooming on both heels
with each miserable step.

His hands shake. Everyone sane
is inside, gathered around tinseled trees
or tables laden with food, probably wondering
who those two wet fools are (*Poor wretches.*

Pitiless storm) but no, my father says,
we have another mile to go before
we can call it a walk. I don't live here
anymore, don't know who does

or who dies here or gives birth in the hospital
ahead of us, who waves down at their children
from the third-floor corner window, the way
my mother held up her fifth baby like

a trophy she'd won at the county fair and there
we are again, lined up and waiting for the whiskered
grille of my father's black Cadillac to nose
up the street and purr into the driveway

where he'll park the car and walk
around to my mother's side, no tremor
in his hand, no hesitation in his step, no,
he can't wait to show us what they've made.

OLD FLAME

Decades after I quit, I still dream
of lighting a cigarette and even
in sleep feel my fingers curve to grip
the filter tip of a Newport, recall
the arc I traced, groove of hand
to lip. Do I miss smoking or the girl
who smoked, who tucked a buck
in the pocket of her cutoff jeans,
so sure the world would buy her Jack
and Coke. Or miss the men who lit
me up—flick of thumb against greased
wheel, first hit igniting tiny white lights
strung nerve to bone, clatter of engine,
rev of cells : oh axons : oh dendrites.

DEPENDING

The rooster no longer cocks
his doodle-doo at me now

that I can't hatch eggs.
Old hen: all fruitless

tubes and bristled
chin. Explaining

the sestina to freshmen
yesterday, I farted. What's

next? Leak of urine, I guess,
unexpected as the day

in eighth grade when I felt
the pinch of a tiny hand

wring my insides: the slide,
the trickle, the long walk

to the desk for a hall pass praying
nothing showed. Years later

when I'd say *Thank you,
Jesus,* or *God damn.*

AN ODE TO
AGING SWIMMERS

This is for you who rise
each day from the dead
of sleep, alarmed

from dreams and bed to bare
your bulk, your sag, and stand
at ocean's edge in baggy suit

of skin, for you who pull
down petaled caps, ignore
the lifeguard's warning

whistle, who run, don't
walk, a song for you
to hum against

the undertow, to sing
as glaciers crumble,
melt, seas heat

piss warm and over-
flow with crap
from continents,

from rivers' mucked-up
effluence, this is for you
who do not fear

what may come, swim
on despite the if,
the when, the after

of after the end
is near.

SAUDADE

*—From the Portuguese: A kind of intense
nostalgia or a constant desire for something that
does not and probably cannot exist*

Like the time your train
tooted out of Utica
three hours late past

a grove of trees wrapped
in white lights, past
the neon signs of a bar

as the last car left
the parking lot,
a black sedan you see

yourself riding in, thigh
to thigh with the blue-jeaned guy
you hooked up with over

whiskey shots and shells of Pabst
at last call, the bass player
for the rock band whose

big hands you'd admired
all night plucking
at his stringed crotch, even

as the jukebox spins out
its last song, even as
a waitress wipes down

the sticky tables with a frayed rag
soaked in club soda, listens
to the train whistle

out of the station, wishing
she were where you are
moving away from her life.

WAITRESS

Wednesdays I waited on women golfers, endless
four-tops just in from playing
a hot eighteen. They drank gallons
of unsweetened iced tea, demanded refills

for free and complained when the brew
wasn't cold or strong enough.
I ran on cans of Tab,
kept a lit Newport perched in the crotch

of a black ashtray, lucky to get
three deep drags between cocktails
and order-ups. The grill cook pointed
a knife at me, threatened to cut off

my tits if I didn't speak up. The bartender
screamed at me for garnishing
a dry Manhattan with a maraschino cherry.
I leaned on the roll warmer and cried.

No one paid attention. Every week, at least,
someone untied her black apron and said,
fuck it, walked out in the middle of a shift
never to be seen again. I dried my eyes.

In the nineteenth hole men slipped bills
in my pocket, eyed the V-neck
of my uniform whenever I set down
another round. An hour after my shift,

I was shit-faced in a bar that didn't card me,
paying for cold Molsons with quarters left
by the lady golfers. I don't remember
walking home on those nights, only

the mornings when I woke to a wink
of coins on the bureau, hours before
I had to punch a clock again. I had nothing
but time and I was rich.

WHAT I'VE LOST

A taste for Southern Comfort. Umbrellas:
two in a week when I was down
to eight bucks in the bank halfway
to payday and rain in the forecast, tail
end of a hurricane that blew
through Cuba, kissed the coast
of Florida and ricocheted into Philly
where its gray buttocks of sky squatted
over us for days. I tied a garbage bag
turban style, swanned past
the row of four-star restaurants
on Walnut Street, imagining I
was a forties movie queen shooting
a scene on a wet set. Next payday, I dropped
seventy bucks on a steak and a bottle
of rosé, something French
and unpronounceable, curly
on the tongue. The sun
was out. I forgot
about rain and sweet
whiskey thick
in my throat.

WONDROUS

I'm driving home from school when the radio talk
turns to E.B. White, his birthday, and I exit
the here and now of the freeway at rush hour

travel back into the past where my mother is reading
to my sister, the part about Charlotte laying her eggs
and dying and though this is the fifth time Charlotte

has died my mother is crying again and we're laughing
at her because we know nothing of loss and its sad math,
how every subtraction is exponential, how each grief

multiplies the one preceding it, how the author tried
seventeen times to read the words *She died alone*
without crying, seventeen takes and a short walk during

which he called himself ridiculous, a grown man crying
for a spider he'd spun out of the silk thread of invention—
wondrous how those words would come back and make

him cry and, yes, wondrous to hear my mother's voice
ten years after the day she died—the catch, the rasp,
the gathering up before she could say to us: *I'm OK.*

CPSIA information can be obtained
at www.ICGtesting.com
Printed in the USA
FSHW020547140222
88242FS

9 780913 785645